HappySad

a book of poems

Bec Moreton

HappySad
a book of poems

First published in Australia by Bec Moreton 2022

Copyright © Bec Moreton 2022
All Rights Reserved

 A catalogue record for this book is available from the National Library of Australia

ISBN: 978-0-6454575-0-6 (pbk)

Typesetting and design by Publicious Book Publishing
Published in collaboration with Publicious Book Publishing
www.publicious.com.au

No part of this book may be reproduced in any form, by photocopying or by any electronic or mechanical means, including information storage or retrieval systems, without permission in writing from both the copyright owner and the publisher of this book.

This is dedicated to everyone who loves me, and everybody who ever thought that I couldn't.

# DENIAL

Melody;

The reflection of the Christmas lights on the dizzy fan gives the illusion of an overly large CD,

    and I think,

        'What music would God play for me, this night?'

Stricken;

There is a thunderstorm gathering on the horizon, the clouds are black and roiling, and the rain will be ruthless.

The dogs are still outside, and they will not come when they're called.

I sit in a chair with the TV on;
when the thunder rolls in, I turn the volume up,
and when the lightning splits the sky, I close the blinds.

I am afraid of a great many things, and I am still young enough to place storms at the top of that very long list.

But sheltered by my dry walls, it is impossible to acknowledge the wrath of nature until the dogs trot back inside and curl up at my feet,
and their fur is wet and matted,
and the smallest pup has a piece of hail in her mouth
that melts into the carpet almost immediately.

Chocolate Fish;

I get angry at my dad a lot.

I don't mean any of it, and I don't know why it happens,
and I always cry afterwards.

And I can never get the words in my apology right,
so I buy him Chocolate Fish,
and we both agree that it's better to pretend that it's alright,
because neither of us know what else to say about it.

Inevitable;

I am sitting on a cold metal seat, and I am waiting.
For what?
    I don't know.

Something is keeping me there, invisible fingers digging
into my shoulders as I peer at the world around me.
Buses pass by.
Some stop and open their doors to me, but I cannot move,
and so I can only watch them vanish into the distance.

The metal seat is surrounded by crystal waters and there
are plants with leaves painted emerald.
Techno-coloured flowers sway in the breeze.
It is beautiful here,
    waiting,
        but it is a cage.

My breath catches.

What am I waiting for?

Another bus stops, doors creaking open.

I beg my legs to move, to run, to escape.
The people on the bus are shouting for me
to hurry up – the driver looks terrified.

What am I waiting for?

I wonder, as the bus dissolves in front of me and the
sapphire water licks closer to my feet, if I am simply
waiting for death to catch up.

    A bus pulls up and opens its doors.

        I go nowhere.

Sage;

"I hate the colour green," I say, at least once a week.

But the problem is that I'm wearing a green shirt,
and there's a green formal dress in my closet,
and there are tiny green flecks in my eyes,
and my friends buy me green crystals.

The problem is that I am so entwined with the colour that it is impossible to see where I end, and green begins.

Vehemence;

The first shot of alcohol is fun,
is familiar.

> The second,
>> The third,
>>> The fourth.

The bottle was full when I started.

By the seventh drink, my mouth is twisting, my eyes
scrunched in displeasure.
The world is blurring around me, heat
grabbing at my throat and my chest,
and it should feel nice, should make me happy,
but you're not laughing anymore, and your glass
sits empty and untouched in front of you,
and suddenly I realise that I'm the only one drinking now.

I call you a quitter.
You call me a drunk.

The eighth shot scorches my tongue because I don't
swallow it properly.

'I can stop,' I say, even as I pour another.
'If I wanted to, I could stop.'

You ask me what I'm running from, and it's only because
I'm nine drinks deep that I can't give you an answer.

Inclination;

I don't remember things properly-
> not in the way that normal people do, anyway.

Things come and go in flashes:
someone's crow-like laugh,
a moment on stage with the lights burning bright,
a microphone that wasn't turned off when I whispered,
a hand on the shoulder,
a hand in my hair,
photos and videos of friends I don't know anymore,
maybe a moment where I was going
to the pool with my cousins.

I have things that I can't remember buying or receiving
or taking,
like necklaces or earrings or figurines or books.
Nail polishes that have long since dried up.

All of these memories I have let slip through my fingers
like grainy sand,
and I don't dare to reach for them,
just in case it starts hurting again.

Negation;

There are warning signs everywhere,
like someone has walked ahead through my life
and planted them in places I cannot avoid.

I close my eyes against them and resign myself to learning Braille.

Minimization;

"Cancer is a great weight loss program," my dad says on Monday, and I laugh, because it's funny.
It's true – our friend has started chemotherapy
and she's shedding her kilos.
She's bed-ridden at the moment, and I joke about how nice it must be to lose weight without having to move.
My mother doesn't laugh with us.

On Tuesday, I snigger and say, "At least she won't have to worry about her roots showing!"
Dad thinks it's funny because she's losing
her hair too quickly now, even though she
said that she'd never let it happen.
My mother purses her lips and looks away.

I get a text on Wednesday, and its me from when I was in hospital for chest pains;
there was a monitor beside me that I wasn't hooked
up to, and it looked like I was flatlining,
and my dad and I thought it was funny.
It's not about her, the text, but my mind goes there anyway,
and I think about medical drama shows,
and calling for a code blue.
I don't text back.

I wake on Thursday and call my mother.
She says that there's not much time
left for our friend, really.
I tell her, "It's okay," and when I hang up, I feel fine.
I shouldn't feel fine, I know that.

I go to work on Friday, and I make it to midday, and then when someone asks me how I am, I can't quite manage to pretend that I'm okay.
I make my confession to my manager in a
too-cold, too-bright meeting room.
I cry all the way home.

Poseidon;

I lose myself in the tumbling ruckus of thoughts,
dashed against the jagged rock cliffs in my
mind by the vicious waves of my grief,
as though I am nothing more than a
flailing weed within my own head.

And I cannot find enough ground to rise above the angry
seas before they haul me under and usher water into my lungs.

Dismissal;

I think if you want to know what I'm feeling,
you need to take out your phone,
and sit there, silently, as the battery runs down to zero.

If you want to know how I'm feeling, you'll watch the power drain, and you'll do absolutely nothing to stop it.

Abandonment;

Dear person,

I say that it doesn't hurt anymore, the memory of you and me.
But your name trembles against my lips when I breathe it out, and my voice creaks and breaks when I admit that I don't know why you left.

I think it must've been your fault – too skittish to be friends with someone like me.

I haven't deleted the messages, because I like to read them to my housemates with a smile,
because I've turned us into a warning story, into a joke, into a maybe and a might-have-been,
because I don't know how else to keep the heartbreak at bay.

Too many people have walked away from me in my lifetime, and you were far from the first,
and you were nowhere near the last,
but you were the most painful.

It keeps me up at night, the wondering.

Why?

> Why?
>> Why?

What did I do?

Nothing.
I did nothing.
You chose to leave me, and that is on you, because I refuse to carry that burden.

I tell people that it doesn't hurt anymore,
you and me,
and I ignore the way the lie tastes sour in my mouth.

Reduction;

It's the sixth call that I've let go to voicemail.

It's midnight, nobody should be calling me, but the phone is trilling on the table next to me,
and I know that if I go to sleep, the
ringtone will follow me,
and I am so tired of running away.

ANGER

Vigilante;

I know that I can do great things,
such great things.
I know that I can be a great person, a kind
person, a person who is loved.

But instead, I swallow my destiny, and I kill her.
I hate her so I beat her, and I poison her,
and she dies holding my hand;
she will never understand why I did it.

My trophy is guilt.
A tidal wave of guilt that starts in my
stomach and crests in my throat,
It suffocates me when I look in the mirror.
She looks back at me.

Tears collect on my chin, gathering in a puddle that defies gravity;
they do not fall.

They gather and gather and gather.

Soon, I have a mask that stifles the screams that are
trapped behind my yellowed teeth.
It is beautiful.
But I am drowning.

I could've been a great person, could've done great things,
but I killed that part of myself so completely that I have
nothing left to give this angry, greedy, lacklustre world.

Commandeer;

How wonderful it will be to die with the heat of battle in our eyes,
the song of battle on our tongues.

How wonderful it will be to die for the blanket desperation to be so helplessly and heartbreakingly human.

Antagonise;

Despite popular belief, I do not *like* being angry.
It's my programming, my baseline, the *safe* choice.
It's the shouted conversations I can still
hear with my bedroom door closed,
the way the slamming kitchen cupboards
don't quite break the icy silence,
sitting in the passenger seat in school uniform
while we follow someone home,
fleeing the twining hallways of the only
house I remember from my childhood,
scrambling to look busy if someone opens my door.

I absorbed that outrage and I pushed it deep down,
and I built myself a ribcage from it,
and I let it grow and swell until it built the
walls around my young and aching heart.

I do not *like* being angry,
but we all do terrible things to survive.

Discrepancies;

The art of knowing myself fades into a ragged tapestry of twilight and doubt;
the stars are blood-stained in the presence of my unknown,
the moon is screaming.

I scream back.

I do not know how to confess that I am not a person;
that I am a rotting pile of hollow bones,
that I am my grief,
that I am afraid of the dark,
that I am lightning trapped beneath the
soft underside of my own tongue.

My teeth are bared in a bitter mockery of a smile,
and my chest aches.

My space-dusted veins glow blue in the night as I dig
fingernails into my arms, searching for the light I once
crammed under my skin;
when I was a child, I stole the crystalline
moonshine right from the night sky.

I am an old soul bound in a young body.

I am a ghost who has forgotten not to get attached to being human.
I am a human who has forgotten what it is like to be alive.

Arrogance;

The number of people I've wanted to punch over my
lifetime is significant,
which is something that has upset a great
deal of friends and family members.

I have abstained, though.

But there is a simmering part of me that carefully notes
down every name,
captures every face,
because one day I will get my revenge,
not through my fists,
but through my success and my happiness.

Heatwave;

Heat curls down my neck, undoing the cool tranquillity of the sleepy night.

It takes me too long to react;
I am sluggish in my comfortable bed,
and my senses are dulled by the
fictitious descriptions of fire,
else I would have noticed it far sooner that I
did, sleep-smothered awareness or not.

Because instead of a roar and a crackle, the fire is a quiet assassin, and it sneaks and creeps like a stalking tiger.

I watch it with an equal measure of silence.

I might have remained there, watching from my bed, had I not been ripped from the pillows and stolen away into the fresh clean air.
Once we're outside, the thunderous
noise descends on me in full-
      the awful cacophony of screams and shouts,
           of snapping and groaning and the screeching
of the fire as it devours my life whole.

Damnify;

Miserable anger grips my chest tight,
holds my heart hostage,
obliterates the sunflower feeling that is my happiness.

This is what I am reduced to – shaking hands and leaky
eyes, a nose that will never dry;
each teardrop trembles against my cheek, holding
all the fury I cannot bring to life with my words.

Dead spiders skitter along my thinning veins,
and their legs are gentle,
but they leave decay in their wake.

    it hurts

        it hurts

            it hurts

Soon, I am breaking in a way that I have only ever seen my
uncle break; it is brutal, messy, loud, and all at once.

Ignorance;

I hate reading about being young.

I am not young, not in the way that matters,
because those that have gone before me have
left me a broken and bleeding world,
and I have endured and endured and endured.

I cannot endure forever,
and I will not endure for the rest of my life.

The age of my bones is not what defines my spirit,
and there is a roaring fire in me that has been stoked
by the injustices of the society I'm bound to.

Abandonment;

Sitting on the time-nibbled couch in the attic of a church,
I consider my therapist.

He's doing that thing I hate, where he sits there and watches me in silence,
where he doesn't give me the answer and
he doesn't tell me what he thinks.
Instead, he's waiting for me to keep talking,
to confess,
to figure out that my anger is the part of me that *loves*.

I shift, kick one leg up over the top of the other, and I say:
"I deserved better."

He says nothing, so I say again, louder:
"I deserved better."

Because I was a child, and I was owed so many things,
    I was owed *love,*
and everybody failed me so completely
that I have spun out of control,
like a little toy spinning top.

And I am angry, and I am upset, and I am tired of succumbing to tears at night;
because I deserved so much better,
and everybody that should've loved me let me down.

My therapist takes a breath, and he says, fiercely:
"Yes you did."

Infinitesimal;

I am tired of being called 'hard to swallow'.

I do not need people to devour my spirit, to inhale my over-emotion until I am barren and naked in front of them, shivering and defenceless and meek.

Where am I to exist?
My corner of the world was taken from me when I was fourteen, sitting in the backseat of a new car, and I was offered no replacement
only a warning to everybody around me.

I am tired of being called 'hard to swallow'
because I am not.
I am small, and pain-soaked, and lonely,
and I am soft beneath my defensive anger.

BARGAINING

Aggrieved;

The dishes won't fit in the *fucking* drying rack.

There are too many, and I can't make them fit, and there are tears in my eyes because I always cry when I'm frustrated.
I want to scream and flail and kick and throw a tantrum,
but instead I mutter a half-hearted prayer
as I continue to cram them together.

If I can just get them to fit, I'll feel better,
and if I feel better, I just might be able to keep going.

Symmetry;

I move through life as though I am in conversation with a deity,
with someone or something that shapes my future,
that decides the weight of my actions,
the worth of my every breath or my every step.

How peculiar that I've never realised the only deity I have to bow to is myself,
the only person I have to justify my existence to is myself.
The only person who gets to choose what
kind of life I'm allowed to live is *myself*.

So, if I'm not happy, and I'm not content,
whose fault is it really?
(Mine,

      Mine,

           Mine.)

And if I'm reduced to begging on both knees in front of the bathroom mirror,
so be it,
if only it means I give myself the chance to *live*.

Reflection;

Mirror, help me,
for I can no longer see myself in your surface

    and I am so very afraid of not existing.

Forsaken;

I am choking on the beautiful flowers that are budding in my throat;
they are made from your betrayal,
they are made from my anguish.

Senseless fire bleeds into a melancholic silence, and at once I am both with and without.

The cold touch of starlight behind my eyes.
The scorching sense of forgotten raking across my teeth.

Please;
Kiss me.
Draw the poison from my lips.
Devour the bloody petals that lay soft
and supple on my tongue.

I have nothing left to offer but that.

Invigorate;

Does my reflection have a name?
Or does she share mine, even as it sits
jagged and bleeding in her mouth.

Sometimes I wonder if she resents me,
for the way I look,
or the way I smile,
or the way I insist on covering it all up anyway.

She might like me better if I was kinder to her,
if I loved her in the way that I crave to be loved,
if I let her exist in her wild and unrestrained way.

My torn fingernails scratch gently at the glass as I reach for her,
as she reaches back,
and my smeared eyes meet hers, and
I laugh and laugh and laugh,
because we're always so tragic together,
      why can't we be happy together too?

Diminish;

Your lips are crusted with dry sand and your tongue is marred with scars.
It's why you struggle to speak, sometimes.
It's why your words are rough.
It's why your voice never soothes my fears.

I ask you now to swallow the ocean.

When the water has loosened your throat and softened your thoughts, I ask of you:
> Please be gentle with me.

I promise that I am trying.

I am just so very tired these days.

Characterized;

I do not believe in a God.

A Force, maybe, some kind of cosmic balance that favours me every now and then,
but not a God.
Never a God.

Except-

I will believe in a God if that's what it takes,
if that's that will keep my loneliness away at night,
If that's what it takes to get someone to stay.

I will trade my barren faith for a gift, for a miracle, for instant gratification,
because I am not patient,
and I will never let someone expect patience of me.

Routine;

I dreamed that my dad died last night;
it was a car crash, quick but brutal,
and the police came knocking on the
door very early in the morning.

When I awoke, tears had dried on my cheeks,
and my fingers itched towards my phone,
where a text sat prettily on the screen.

> *'I love you. Have a good day at work today.'*

Parents are never supposed to outlive their children,
but there is nothing in me that is strong
enough to survive if I lose them.

I beg-

> Take me. Take me first and leave them in peace.

What-If;

What if I had been born a boy;
with short blond hair and a diagnosed attention disorder,
with an attitude that people found
funny instead of strange,
with a loud laugh that might've been endearing,
without the emotional outbursts the ruined so many
of the good things I might've had as a child.

What if I'd been gifted a sibling,
and what if it had been a younger brother,
and I'd been forced to give love as
easily as I expect to receive it,
and finally I might've had someone who'd
done the things I'd always wanted to do,
but who'd stolen the attention I already fight so
hard to keep, who might have overshadowed me.

What if I could live my life without ADHD;
could focus on one task easily, without
risk of numerous distractions,
could sleep without constantly playing noises and songs,
could stick to deadlines and be proactive
and make my sentences make sense,
even if I lost my beautiful spiderweb of thoughts.

What if I never survive anybody that I know;
because what if I cannot bear that
burden upon my shoulders.

Foreboding;

What must I change within myself so that people start staying?

Because I have lost and loved and lost again, and the loneliness is devouring me whole,
so I ask again,

>What is it that I must do, what is it that I must say,

>>So that someone might want to keep me beside them?

Fealty;

I promise that I will never do it again,
that I will dim my voice and soothe my temper,
that I will not talk just to talk,
that I will be easier to be around, easier to love.

I swear that I will be someone to be proud of,
that I will achieve things that people expect me to achieve,
that I will start winning again,
that I will give so much of myself that you have to love me.

I vow that I will be easier to manage,
that I will keep my messiness to myself,
that I will trap my misery behind my discoloured
teeth so that others will not suffer with me,
that I will do more because I know that acts of
service don't make me feel cheap like words do.

I will be so much better.

Please believe me.

DEPRESSION

Incapable;

Oxygen is a useless weight in my chest;
It pleads with my lungs,
presses again my heart,
taps along my bones.

I am heavy with it – so unbearably heavy with it.
So I breathe out

        out

            out

until my ribs squeeze and creak and moan in protest.

Inevitably and far too soon, I breathe back in.
My body sags to the ground, my knees
snapping under the pressure.
My head is pounding.

I can't keep going like this.

I breathe out again.

    Then in.

        Then out,
           out,
               out.

Slipping;

Sometimes I think that I am the reason that all the bad things happen.
That I was born wrong,
with something *broken* in me,
and that is why I will never be satisfied
with everything I already possess.

Cataclysmic;

Lying in bed with stinging eyes, and I'm thinking,
'I don't like it here anymore.'

Penalty;

I cannot make you understand why I get tattoos,
because you have not felt the sting
of metal against your skin
or the fizzy demand for marks in
places that are hard to see.

I do not go looking for pain – that is what is important.
I do not seek it, and though it often comes to
me intending comfort, I turn it away.
I do not need it, do not desire it, do not embrace it.

But, not unlike a fantasy story, I need to be bound to this body.

Because I do not think that I was meant to be stranded here,
ill-fitting and discorded,
in a body that feels both far too much and far too little.

I am not satisfied by living, by existing;
I seek permanent scars to stitch myself to this vessel,
to keep myself whole and safe and present.
As though my soul, my spirit, needs to be trapped
here so that it will not take me wandering
to a place that I cannot return from,
that nobody can follow me to.

I do not know how to make the words leave my tongue
when you show me those sad eyes,
because shame burns hot and tight in my throat,
and I know that you would not understand,
that you would send me away.

I do not think I would survive being sent away.

I am barely holding on as it is.

Wholeheartedly;

I can't bring myself to feel anymore,
because too many times I have been betrayed by my heart,
betrayed by my desires,
and if it happens one more time, I
fear that I will never recover,
will never be whole again.

I can't bring myself to feel anymore,
because love is synonymous with pain.

Wistful;

My old bedroom had six walls;
I would trace the hexagonal shape of the ceiling with my eyes during the days when I couldn't get out of bed.

My new bedroom also has six walls,
but the roof is not a hexagon.
My furniture seems to fit better, though.

I could not take my cat with me when I moved out, and so there is nobody who will lay with me when I sob into my pillow.
I miss her with all my heart.

I stuck glow-in-the-dark stars to my bookcase,
because I miss the ones I had when I was a child,
and I'm still afraid of the dark,
and they give me something to look at when
my head doesn't want to leave my pillow, and I
cannot bear to get out from under the covers.

Echolocation;

I stare at the Ace of Spades in my hand because it's my favourite card, and it's supposed to be worth something in the game we're playing.

What game are we playing?

Someone explained the rules to me, I think, but I don't remember them,
don't know what to do with the cards in my hand.
It's my turn, and people are staring,
but I don't know,

    I don't know,

        I don't know-

I play the Ace of Spades.

Someone says something to my left, but I don't hear the words.
Hands sweep up the scattered cards, and
fingers pry the others from my grip.
Have I won?
Have I lost?

Do I care?

I am dealt another hand, and when I pick up the cards to look at them, I see the Ace of Spades.

Overwhelming;
Somewhere, a clock is ticking.
I ache for the day it falls silent.

Composition;

An orchestra plays mournful eulogies in the gloom of the midnight hours;
I sit with my head bowed,
my back hunched,
denying myself the comfort of the bed I sit in,
and I listen.

The music does not ease the hollow weight that yawns behind my ribcage and threatens to swallow my heart whole.
The music does not ease my sore and gritty eyes.

Instead, weeping violins pay homage to the blankness within me,
gentle clarinets give shape to the greyed
smudge that might be my haggard soul,
bittersweet cellos capture me, paint me, in all of my grief.

I am a beautiful song when I am engulfed by my tragedies.

Moonbeam;

The dark night folds me into its arms as I walk to my car.

"Where are you going?" My housemate had asked.

The only answer I had been able to offer had been, "Away."

I get in the car,
feel the pedals beneath my feet,
the steering wheel gripped tight by my fingers,
and as I start to drive, I wonder if tonight will
be the night that I don't make it back home.

Ruinous;

I wanted to write a poem about angels,
and how I used to dream that they were real.
I don't believe in them, and I'm not religious,
but I was so unbearably lonely that I would
imagine them flocking to me at night,
imagine them holding me close and singing me to sleep.

I wanted to write a poem about angels,
       but I'm so much older now,
              and I cannot seem to find the words.

Disconnection;

There is something about not looking both ways before
crossing the street that is dangerously gleeful;
if someone were to hit me and I were to
die, I would not be held accountable,
and in my misery, I'm vindictive enough to revel
in taking someone else down with me.

A shame, then, that nobody ever reaches to pull me back
from the curb.

A shame, then, that they first let me cross before lashing
their tongues down my back and leaving me shaking and quiet,
without ever wondering why it is that I'm
not afraid to take that first step.

I do not know how many more times I can cheat Death
before it comes looking for me,
and though I might embrace it like a lover,
I may lose my chance to escape the
responsibility of my demise.

Impending;

I greet Sadness like an old friend.

It seeps into the woven threads of my clothes,
swirls in the yawning cavity of my mouth,
teases its way down my throat and into my lungs.
It curls around my heartbeat and scratches
a fingernail along my ribcage.

The smoky taste of anti-happy stains my tongue ashen and
I cannot wash it away with faux, cherry-flavoured good days.

There is much despair within me.
It will never go away.

ACCEPTANCE

Doppelganger;

I do not know how not to be who I am:
how not to thread words through my teeth
and taste the history behind each syllable,
how not to brush my fingertips over the world and
delight in the smear of existence left on my skin,
how not to exist in a way that is entirely
foreign to everybody but me.

I do not know how to relinquish the battered and aching parts of me:
how to swim to shore with tired arms and rest on warm sands and finally allow a god to give me the answer instead,
how to surrender the ghosts that linger in
my room and breathe their stories into the
crown of my head when I am sleeping,
how to forget the swirling bruises I have
pressed into my skin and buried in blank
ink and the buzz of a tattoo needle,
how to give up everything that has become of me.

I do not know how to apologise to the universe for taking up too much space, for breathing too much air, for making too much noise.

I do not think the universe minds, though, because it, too, remembers what it is like to be so breathtakingly young.

Resonate;

There is a young girl who lives in my chest, and she is many things.

She's headstrong,
and empathetic,
and eager,
and willing to do everything she can to help.

She is not weak.

But she is overly self-critical,
and she is afraid of the wrong things,
and I cannot help her because damage nurtures damage and the cycle will begin anew.

"I'm ruining you," I say to her one night, while I cradle her in my palms.

She blinks up at me, so familiar, and says, "Only because you love me."

Blanket;

My housemate's dogs look at me like they know something about me that I don't know about myself.

It's unsettling,
makes me uncomfortable sometimes.

But then they choose my bed some nights,
and steal my covers,
and it squashes the heart beating feebly in my chest,
because if they know about the horrors I'm harbouring,
then they are *choosing* me, and they are *choosing* to stay.

Unwoven;

I write about my own thoughts so much that I forget there is more to me than the happenings of my own mind;
I forget about matters of the heart.

And sometimes, I proceed through life as though I am free of flawed humanity.
It is an untruth.

I would like to believe that I am without

>greed,

>>jealousy,

>>>envy,

But I cannot lie forever.

I say that my heart is a tapestry of
love, but here is my secret:

>My heart is a tangled knot of the colour green, and everything that it stands for.

Burden;

No single person has been told the depth of my struggling,
and that is a choice that I have made,
and that is a choice that I will stand by until
the day I am sure that I am in love,
and that I am loved in return.

Until that day, though, I will split my lake of sadness into thin streams,
and I will give each stream to a person,
so that they may hold me up until I
am able to stand on both feet,
because there is nothing wrong with asking for help.

Filth;

My room will never stay clean for more than a week,
and I will never not be ashamed of it.

Exceptional;

My therapist, in our first session, asked me what I wanted to get out of therapy,
and I told him that I needed to find a
way to co-exist within myself,
to be able to live with the darker parts
of me that I couldn't carve out.

He might've looked sad for a moment.

But I think I might love that part of me now, just a little bit,
enough to treat it a little gentler,
enough to treat *myself* a little gentler.

Recompense;

One day, I will be able to sit down with my mother and tell her the entire truth.
She will cry, and I will cry, and she'll
ask me what she did wrong,
but I can promise that she did nothing,
that I was brought into this world with an insistence
on secrets and a sensitivity for other people,
and there was no way that I could confess my
troubles without her thinking she was the victim.

And she will read these writings, one day,
and I will receive a hug so warm and tight,
and there will be tears then too.

Because my mother loves me, and I love her too, and one day, that will finally be enough for me.

Decayed;

She gives me dried roses one night, while we stand beside her car and delay saying goodbye.

They smell beautiful,
and I love them, I love them, I love them.
I say: "Thank you for the dead flowers."
She says: "They reminded me of you."

And I don't know how to tell her that it's the first time I can laugh at that kind of joke without immediately wanting to cry.

Infinite;

I did not plan my life past high school.

I knew which career I would go into, and I knew how to
manage finances, and I went looking for apartments,
and some might call that life,
but I don't.

Because I have felt nineteen years old since the second day
of grade nine,
and life has always held little joy,
and I let the people around me convince me
that self-sufficiency was the key to living.

My housemates took me out to a pub in the city two months ago,
and that-

>   *that-*
>
> >   was living.
>
> And finally, I think I might want to try it.

Bittersweet;

I will never fully heal the wounds that I received when I was a child, and I will never be able to prevent getting hurt as I continue to grow.

There will still be nights where I lay in bed and cry as Hans Zimmer plays quietly from the speaker,
and there will still be last-minute car drives with the stereo cranked up and my hands clasped tightly on the wheel,
and there will still be a deep and gouging scar deep inside my chest where my heart once tried to escape my ribcage.

But there will be peace within me, sometimes,
and suddenly it will be easier to exist,
to breathe in.

There will be days where sunshine upon my skin will feel like a blessing, and I will chase the bumblebees with every ounce of joy I felt when I was too young to know loneliness, and the love that leaks steadily from my veins
won't feel like shackles around my wrists.

And there will be days where I'm so in love with living that I cannot fathom why I ever wanted to give it up,
and it will be on those days that I am
so breathlessly proud of myself,
that my parents and my friends are proud of me,
that I might just start to believe I'll make it.

Portraiture;

My housemates did a painting day while I was working, once,
and created two masterpieces,
and I will never be able to articulate how those
emotion-soaked canvases made me feel.

Because one was soft and sweet and lovely;
colour-pop clouds drifting lazily along the bottom,
the moon painted simple and lovely,
the stars a smattered freckling across
an uneven black background.
So beautiful in its simplicity and imperfectness.
The other…

>   *Oh*, the other.

It hangs in my room, the second painting,
peeled softly out of the hands of its
hesitant and overly critical creator,
and it steals the breath from my lungs and the thoughts
from my head whenever my wandering eyes land upon it.

I have no words to describe it.
Perhaps something akin to wistfulness
or nostalgia or longing.
Perhaps something akin to healing.

YOU

Communication;

"If I asked you to love me, would you?"

> *I have served you my heart upon a silver platter,*
> *held it out with bloody and shaking hands.*
> *You have owned my love since we first met, and*
> *though I would try should you ask me, I cannot give*
> *you anything more.*
> *I have nothing else to give.*

"If I asked you to sacrifice for me, would you?"

> *I have already surrendered too much in your name,*
> *and yet, against all rationality,*
> *yes, I would give up everything else that I covet, should*
> *you ask it of me.*

"And if I asked you not to hurt me, would you?"

> *We cannot love each other without pain,*
> *because there is something jagged and broken in the*
> *way we hold each other,*
> *there is something dangerous in the knowledge that*
> *only the two of us can survive this twisted, bitter*
> *relationship.*
> *I will offer you all of me, will scoop out my insides and*
> *offer them to you without question,*
> *but this, love you without hurting you, I will not do.*
> *This I cannot do.*

Olympus;

I am not so bold as to call you a goddess, but I cannot
deny that you are larger than this life;
you are built from moonbeams
and discarded wishes
and half-forgotten dreams.

Your ribcage contains dragons,
your throat reeks of fire

When the thunder roars, you are the one who roars back,
untamed by the deafening display of a pain so old
that time itself cannot stand to remember it,
and you bask gloriously in the tears of the old gods.

Lightning crackles in your eyes, and when you look at me,
my knees tremble in fear of the centuries-old rage I see.

You know that the world does not allow perfection to exist,
and you wear that knowledge with a smile because
      you are beautiful, despite it.

Advice;

I can tell you this:

Take inspiration from your suffering.
If it is drowning you, then at least make
your last breaths worth painting.

Poisonous;

I see you when I close my eyes,
not in any form that is possible on this plane of existence,
but as a flash of white light,
a strike of lightning against my shut eyelids.

See, you haunt me, and no matter where I go, I cannot
outrun the thought of you.
You live in my dreams, in my breath, in my heartbeat:
festering inside my veins like an untreated wound,
leaking venom into my blood until there is
no part of me that you don't know.

Fantasia;

There is magic in the sting of your lips, pressed against mine, and I am reminded that loving you is a war.

The smudge of my lipstick on your mouth is the only proof I have that I hurt you.

Wretched;

There is broken glass in every word we say to each other.

And I'm angry because you keep trying to leave,
angry because you keep dancing just outside my reach,
angry because I know that if you go somewhere
that I can't follow, then there will be nothing
left to hold me back from that edge.

I am angry because I learned to covet the things I wanted
when I was sitting in Math class in grade nine, watching for
updates as a government decided whether I could get married,
and I love you, and I need you, and I want to marry you,
and I'm angry because I'm so scared
that I'm not going to be able to.

You are angry because you have given so much of yourself to me,
have dedicated all of who you are,
sacrificed all of who you will be,
because you love me, you love me, you love me.

You are angry not because you're scared, but because you
are tired, and you are giving up.
You are angry because I'm not listening
to everything that you don't say,
because I am still listening to the ghost-voices of everyone
who ever said I was wrong for *loving* someone.

So, there is glass in every word we say,
because we are angry, and we're hurting,
and one day, we will kill each other.

And I am so, so sorry.

Plaintive;

You exist in a certain kind of way,
and when I see the sun glide it's rays through your hair,
I understand that my love for you will crush me,
and your love for me was never real.

Unravel;

You look different in the moonlight.

Where I expected the moon to sharpen, it has softened,
and where I expected you to appear ethereal,
I simply see you as startingly human.

Desirous;

Do you know that there is an ocean named after you?
'The Sea of Atlas' they called it in the olden days, but I
think it's just the Atlantic now.
I suppose it's fitting – the New World swallows myths like you,
and steps on your brilliance until it's as broken and
smothered and muddy as the rest of us.

You shoulder the weight of eons, bear the brunt of dying magic,
and you do it without smudging the drying paint on
your face, without cracking the frame around you,
and the thin marble that coats your
physical form stretches as you move,
as you settle the globe against your shoulders.

I think you've been sleeping for a long time, curled around
that last flickering ember of the Old Religions,
waiting for the day we stop destroying
ourselves and the things we love,
and when we start to return to the dirt we came from, you
will awake, and you will release the world from your hands,
and open your eyes to gaze upon your new kingdom.

Kintsugi;

Your limbs are stitched on by molten glass, red-orange in its heat, and it reminds me of the Japanese art of fixing broken things with gold.

Hourglass;

You think that I have surrendered to my dreams, which is
why you dare to brush your trembling fingertips against
my cheek,
and I hold my breath just so,
because you have always claimed that your hands
are weapons that know no gentleness,
that your knuckles have tasted too much
blood to ever treasure unbroken skin,
and your nails have been bitten to the quick so you
won't ever hurt yourself when you make a fist.

I do not know why tonight is different:
unless it isn't,
unless you do this most nights when
I am not awake to be aware,
so you know that this tender side to you remains a
perfectly kept secret that cannot be used against you,
that I will never know that you treasure me so,
and you can ensure that I never ask it of you.

We have not co-existed well in our waking hours lately.
I do not know if I should blame you and your
uncontrollable anger for spewing such hateful accusations,
or if I should blame myself and my defensive, misery-
fuelled retorts that speak only to my argumentative
nature and not to how much I love you.

But now, right now in this second, while the cloak of night
grants you a moment of invisibility and peace,
you touch me, and it does not hurt,
and I might, for one fragile moment, be able to fool
myself into thinking you could love me too.

Fleeting;

My darling, we are nothing more than passion that fancied itself a fire.